Words for Flying

✈✈✈

CHRIS ABBATE

FUTURECYCLE PRESS
www.futurecycle.org

*Cover artwork, vintage Leonard da Vinci inventions; author photo by Sharon
Penn; cover and interior design by Diane Kistner; Avenir text and titling*

Library of Congress Control Number: 2022900856

Published by FutureCycle Press
Athens, Georgia, USA

ISBN 978-1-952593-25-3

To the men and women who shaped me

Contents

Words for Flying

His prayer at takeoff,
the man in the seat next to me—
the practiced crossing of himself
before kissing his thumbnail—
reminds me of my childhood mantra,
Lord willing,
at any mention of the future.
A divine safety net.
A worn path of petition.

The first time I flew as a child,
I gripped an armrest with one hand
and rosary beads with the other.
My brother walked freely
up and down the aisle
as if we didn't need God to fly.

Before touchdown, the man
crosses himself again.
The wing flaps rise as we brake,
reveal braided arteries of hydraulics.
Our bodies lurch forward,
hover for a moment in our chairs,
incidental to gravity and lift,
thrust and drag.

The man glances at me, relieved.
Neither of us has words for flying,
and a turbine needs no intercession.
More likely, we are the plane's prayer,
suspended between body and spirit,
ignorance and understanding.

How else to explain
our tearing through the stratosphere
at six hundred miles per hour—
intentions climbing, soaring,
peering over the edges of our lives—
then gliding back to Earth,
barely feeling a thing?

To the Man Who Stole My Book at a Book Fair

A poem is an anonymous gift to an anonymous audience.
~ Leo Connellan, Poet Laureate of Connecticut 1996-2001

What would you risk for poetry?
Your clandestine hand?
Your slippery fingers?
I wonder if you are more courageous
for stealing than I am for writing.
Or if I should be flattered
by your boldness.

In Afghanistan, women write
subversive two-line poems called landays—
Pashto word for short, poisonous snakes.
An Afghan woman, Zarmina,
burned herself alive
after her brothers beat her
for having written them.

Perhaps the writing instructor
who told me there is no such thing
as an original idea was right.
Those poems were never mine
to begin with. They were just thoughts
that simmered while mowing the lawn
or vacuuming. Footprints
from the back and forth of a day.

Think of them as an arrangement
of mental furniture, a room
I have reserved for you
to toss your worries
over the back of a chair
and to sit for an afternoon.

Or think of them as a match
cast to your presumptions.

When your fingertips
skim those pages,
may you feel
ever so slightly
what it is to burn.

Neighborhood Men

Neighborhood men talk in driveways, over the hoods of SUVs,
they talk as if they need a piece of steel between them.

They talk in clichés, spit consonants, curse like car engines starting.
They stop their lawnmowers to talk, fold themselves over to pull a stray weed.

They talk about the thing they just bought, how much they saved,
they like to compare their stuff to your stuff, explain why you need the stuff
      they have.

Neighborhood men talk like tools in the garage, potential energy,
they talk about what they will do someday when they have the time.

They talk about tomorrow or next week, they say *we should* to each other,
as in going out for a beer or playing golf some Saturday. But until then

they will hang like shovels in perfect rows. They will be reliable and stiff.
They will wake up, get dressed and drive to work, and at the end of the day

they will pull into the driveway, go inside, turn on the news, and ponder
the hard lines of houses and yards and sidewalks, the ones the neighborhood

seemed to draw around them when they weren't paying attention.
They will think of ways to bend the lines into a shape they can describe.

The shape of diligence, of winches, and chain saws, and trees they used to climb.
One that resembles the question their wives are always asking.

The shape of contentment. A thought that vanishes somewhere between the
      alarm clock
and the shower. A shape they could fall in love with if only it had a name.

Dogs

After his fight with the kid up the street,
Patrick and I walk back to his house

and sit under the glow of an autumn tree.
Next time, he will carry a rock in his pocket

to punch through the hard exterior
of Matthew's cheekbone. I didn't understand their fighting,

how they quickly turned into dogs,
how their faces tightened as if they were looking

into a sun, as if it were always too bright.
One winter, I threw a snowball

that exploded against Patrick's temple.
He jumped on my back and began punching me,

but I couldn't bring myself to hit him.
From a distance, my older brother watched us wrestle and release.

As he walked me over the hardened snow toward our kitchen light
where our mother was preparing dinner, he said,

When you're fighting, there are no rules.
You've got to kick his ass good. You've got to kill him.

Smash It Up

Gonna scream and shout to my dying breath
Gonna smash it up 'til there's nothing left
~ The Damned

Lance is taking out his father again
in the form of a long-handled sledgehammer
through the windshield and doors
of his Ford Pinto.

Maple trees stand watch,
stiffly, silently in the yard
while he, bare-chested
in cut-off jeans, hoists the metal block
above his head like a god.

I understood how his father
could make you feel like
smashing something—
the way he scolded me
if I hadn't delivered his morning
newspaper by five-thirty.

Most fathers have a way
of guiding their sons along,
but Lance's seemed to have filled
his son's head with explosives.

Once, Lance used his slingshot
to fire a hex nut at my brother
as he sat on the stone wall along our driveway.
Perhaps it was giving a warning
about what boys like Lance
were capable of, because,
until the moment the nut lodged in his thigh,
my brother swore it made a sound like a scream.

Revenge Enough

Some boys didn't like
how he kept to himself,

how he circled the basketball pole
during recess, kicking gravel.

They didn't like how he tried
to befriend them once,

how he smiled too much
and asked too many questions.

I remember their irritation,
on three occasions how they cut

the air with their fists,
splitting his chin on the playground,

his head shooting back,
a deer in the crosshairs.

And I remember them getting away with it,
boys for whom violence was elemental,

who learned to love in reverse, who crossed
themselves beneath the crucifix in our classrooms.

I saw a picture of the boy today, years later,
retired Air Force captain, slight smile, metal gaze,

and recall how he never retaliated,
how his resilience was revenge enough.

Chemistry

Sister Marguerite hands our chemistry tests back
from highest to lowest score
and I'm at the end again.

She looks down at me
as I approach her foot-high platform.
She is more width than length,
more neutron than electron,
a clash of white face
framed by a black habit and veil,
globular glasses resting on pillow cheeks
and round ankles rooted into thick-soled shoes.

She shakes her head three times
in practiced measure,
evoking thoughts of her Lord—
his temptation in the desert,
Peter denying he ever knew him,
the days before he came back to life.

But there is no hope
for my resurrection.
My paper has been flogged red.
Another mess I've made.
Another sin of omission.
When I reach for it,
she purses her lips
as if there is something more
I should be sorry for.
Some inherent ability
God withheld from me at birth.
An ineptitude to balance chemical equations,
to memorize the atomic mass of magnesium.

As I walk back to my desk
under the gaze of classmates,
I wish I knew that someday
I would understand equilibrium—

that my hands contained
the residue of dead stars,
that Sister Marguerite and I
were as old as the universe itself,
that the same chemical reaction produced
the humiliation she handed down
and the grace I would learn from it.

Odd Camaraderie

It was a gesture of irony,
a universal directive

among the crude space of men
huddled inside a conference room,

learning a new software
that had no syntax

for busting a co-worker's chops
about his advanced age.

And, with the air still damp with satire,
the instructor's back turned,

as if on cue,
the flash of a middle finger

from the perpetrated to the perpetrator.
Then, a ripple of laughter

at the shock of retribution,
a juxtaposition of denotation and connotation

upsetting this field of certainty—
ifs and thens, dos and ends—

with the unspoken language of boys
who twist insults into arrows,

meld barbs into shields—
our everyday armaments

and a consummation
of odd camaraderie.

Uncle Jerry

for Gerald Rago

The day before you died, I tickled you.
I thought you needed cheering up;
after eight years of living with my family,
you dreaded having to go to a nursing home.

I charted my teenage growth spurts
against your four-foot frame, the hump
along your upper back like a question mark,
your deformity a public curiosity.

You made me feel bigger than I was,
but isn't that what boyhood is about,
to someday stake one's place
among the monoliths of men?

I helped you undress after your arms had lost their range,
and climbed into the shower in my bathing suit
to wash the parts you couldn't reach,
the soft parts I imagined once held muscle and form.

I remember the summer we took you on a family trip to Maine.
You sat in the kitchenette one night and sobbed
because, at seventy-five, you had never been on vacation.

We were told Jesus said that whatever we do
to the least of us, we do to him.
But how were we to know you were the Jesus we had been looking for?
That, for every year you were shunned, you collected a cup
and were finally filling one of them with rain?

Catching the Fish

A fish in my tank
is dying of old age,
of all things,
having lived six years,
her underside sunken in now,
her body blemished,
fins like tattered flags
of surrender.
I want to save her
a shred of dignity—
as dignified as a net
and toilet can be—
but she eludes me,
whips her delicate
blue body
and slips between
stacks of slate.

The others will sense
her weakness
and will pick
at her without mercy.
I know.
I have endured job layoffs
and high school.
I have seen how some of us eat
each other—
first the hands and arms,
then the stomach,
and finally the eyes.

The next morning,
the fish wills herself
to the surface for food,
her miraculous little jaw
still hinging
open and closed.

She seems lost
in some aqueous eternity,
a secret flow.
She is at the center
of the universe,
as much as anything else.
As much as me.
And who's to say each of us isn't?
As if we knew where the center was.

Later I slide
the net toward her again,
but she escapes.
This is as good as it gets,
she seems to say,
and I am hard-pressed
to explain her grit.
God, let me be like that.

Ode to A Couch

A neighbor and I drag you
down two flights of stairs,
grunt against your heft,
a dying animal to be euthanized.
We turn your rigid body
gently around corners
as if not to hurt you,
as if you could feel pain.

Set along the curb,
you look displaced,
beige floral pattern
against oil-spotted asphalt,
no longer defined
by the things that once surrounded you.
No longer a haven
for Sunday afternoon naps
and late-night TV shows.

When you were new,
I wicked the slightest drop of water
that fell on you;
fluffed your cushions every night
as if apologizing for laying
the weight of my body
on you so shamelessly.

We are careful at first
with those we love.
The cautious dance,
the asking permission.
Then, reaching the stage
of familiarity, tolerating
the other's idiosyncrasies.

I wish I could love
the way a couch loves,
to be unconditionally inviting,
nothing but giving.

And to be loved back
despite my shortcomings.
My loose threads
and creaking frame.
My flattened edges.

Hitting the Deer

This isn't about hitting the deer
or pulling the car over
along a dark shoulder of road
to check the bumper
while a few feet away
you hear the deer's alien gasp for air,
notice the sudden rise and fall
of its belly.

This is about perspective,
about seeing the forest
for the thin vein of asphalt
you had laid claim to.
It is about how far
you have strayed
from the circle
and the boxes
you have taken shelter in.

This is about scarcity and abundance,
how you could live a day,
a lifetime,
without having one authentic moment,
how you have gone and surrounded yourself
with every fake thing.

The eye of the deer holds everything
you haven't considered—
the vast aloneness of birth,
the frailty of belief,
the varying distances of stars
against the flat canvas of night.

This is about what could have become of you
had you avoided the deer.
Another constellation slipping from memory.
Leaves falling into sameness around a common tree.
Green fading into blue.

Canine Study #1: A River, Flowing

I've stopped asking the dog
about his day.

Instead, I ponder the moon
while he empties his bladder
over a crescent of periwinkle
around the mailbox.

I carry him inside each night
and hold him,
to know what it is like
to feel everything.

Tomorrow, I will commit the original sin
of self-consciousness
and will crease the fine tablecloth
of a new day.

To me, eternity is like a car,
passing,
but to him, it is a river,
flowing.

No wonder his life is so short.
All that ecstasy.
I couldn't bear it.

School Zone

At twenty-five miles per hour
it's sudden weightlessness,
a forced repose
compared to the rush of throughways.
There is time to make eye contact
with the crossing guard
and wave back. Time to count
the magnolias framing the entrance.

When he drove me to school,
Dad would sing opera,
an inflated version of *O Sole Mio*,
a coffee cup balanced on his knee,
shouting at anyone who held him up.

Lately, he asks when can I visit him in Florida
to help clean out his garage and shed.
He says he is slowing down.
The lights are getting dim, he tells me.
And *I'm not going anywhere, but I'm going somewhere.*

I have disobeyed speed limits since I learned to drive.
I have mistaken haste for productivity
and have been moving faster than I was meant to.
But these shortcomings I cleverly disguise,
like the false reverence with which I pass this school.

I think about how much grace aging requires.
How someday, it would be nice to accomplish nothing
and wonder what became of all the doing I did.
To collect hours like years
and learn to float, to hover,
admiring all the bright objects passing by.

Upside-down

Because he had lived eighty years
right-side up—
having shouldered marriage,
mortgage and children,
keeping afloat the glass ball
of responsibility and obligation—
to be upside-down
in his overstuffed shed
after digging through tote boxes
looking for Christmas lights
was quite undignified,
as was his calling out for help
to a canyon of storage units.

Poetic justice
was how he described it to me—
a man undone
by the accumulation of his life,
of things he had once deemed necessary.

He explained how he broke free
by stirring the air with his legs,
his thighs still solid
from his days playing first base,
a variation of the man he discarded
when he assumed the title
of my father.

But that moment of desperation
in the belly of the fish,
did it feel like death to him?
Or was it the distillation that occurs
when we come to the end
of ourselves?
When all that we have is lost
and we discover the rare vessel
buried under layers of flesh?

Last Request

As you went one night last week
so went your lawn,
and while your family drove north
to bury you,
it stood to reason that I push
my mower down the sidewalk
to take care of your business.
I imagined you on the porch
in your plastic chair
with the Army green cushion,
pinching a Marlboro in one hand,
a scotch in the other
watching me labor back and forth,
not minding the ways we kill ourselves,
or the way grass grows
regardless of whether we observe it,
or how clouds unravel themselves into shadows
pretending to be bigger than they are.

I heard that on the night you died
you asked your wife to hold you
before slipping through her hands,
the kite of you floating
through the bedroom ceiling,
its arched tail snaking
between the fan blades.
I'd like to think our last request
is for something to hold onto.
A hand mirror,
old photographs.
Or perhaps to revisit the vantage point
of a porch,
to remind ourselves that we are greater than clouds,
as if anything actually belonged to us,
as if everything were really ours.

Fun to Die

When I was a toddler, my brother saved me
from drowning in a bathtub.
Another time, he pulled me back from an oncoming truck.

In college, my friend fell asleep while driving.
We went sixty into a guardrail
and the seat belt cast a bruised rainbow across my chest.

Today, as they pass me on the sidewalk,
a boy asks his father
if it is fun to die.

He is walking ahead of his father,
holding his hand.
A tugboat towing a barge.

I have heard that impermanence
is the source of joy,
but maybe there is some strange comfort in dying too.

Life, like an amusement park ride,
stomach in the throat, squealing.
And death the letting go, finally, of the bright balloon

we have been holding all day,
and grinning as it rises, the hand relaxing again,
because there is nothing left to carry.

After the House Is Demolished

After the house is demolished
for the new highway,
there is only debris—
pink, fibrous innards,
strewn femurs and fingers,
its bones pointing every which way.
It is a body blown apart,
a massacre of serenity,
a casualty of migration.
Loss on top of loss.

I'd like to make sense
of other things
that have been destroyed
by the fires, floods, and murders
I've seen on the evening news.

My father says he will be
cremated when he dies.
I imagine him in a pile of ash.
His shoulders, chin, and eyes.
His knees I would balance on
some nights after dinner.
His laugh lines,
his inflection,
his sayings.

He used to hand a red rose
to every woman
after Mass on Christmas Eve.
What happens to gestures
of kindness like this?
To the disparate parts
of this thing I call *Dad*?
A perfect array of petals.
A stem and thorns.

God, Bowling

When the thunderclap was a cosmic crash, when it shook
the foundation of the house until the vibration rippled upstairs

to the room my brother and I shared,
we called it a strike.

And when it sounded like a train that had passed,
a rumbling in the distance, the sky merely clearing its throat,

we admitted that even God sometimes threw a gutter ball.
The only picture of my grandfather I remember

is him in a suit and tie holding a bowling ball to his heart,
eyeing pins at the end of a lane.

His obituary from 1959 read, *Giuseppe Stefano, Expert Duckpin Bowler;*
not what my mother had told me about him—

farmer, immigrant, factory worker, gardener—
but rather, what I imagined him to be—

herder of storm clouds, gatherer of sky,
hands that made thunder.

Uncle Frank

for Frank Casale

Not really my uncle, but a man who lived across the street from us,
who twirled a toothpick between his lips like a small baton
and spoke as if his throat were lined with sandpaper.

He was one of those old Italians who didn't take crap from anyone,
who smelled like smoked bacon and didn't have kids or family that we knew of.
So, we made him part of ours, because we had uncles and aunts to spare,

and what's one more? Especially one with a lake house he invited us to in
        the summer
where he showed me how to cast a line and remove a hook,
how to start an outboard and steer it back to the dock.

I never saw him swim, or smile, for that matter,
and his favorite remark was *You don't show me too much.*
It was as if he had been watching me closely,

as if he were concerned about how I would get along someday,
when I figured he couldn't care less about a kid
who tried to show appreciation for a man who would eventually drift

into a forgotten corner of our family's history.
I don't know what became of him, how he died or when,
except to recall his remark that my father and I say to each other now in tribute.

The brashness of it. How it toed the line between ridicule and affection.
Some people are fearless that way.
Some people have a strange way of saying *I love you.*

Big Eater

To my father, it was a mark of distinction, the sign of having become a man.
He's a big eater, he'd say to my mother as she handed him dishes to dry
after the dinner guests had left. It was strange, his fascination
with men who could eat a lot, men who didn't simply satisfy their hunger,

but had the gall to exceed it. He was especially intrigued by men who
    outweighed him
by one hundred pounds and would remind me to treat these men with respect.
Why one hundred? I thought, except that it was a round number that implied
    a lot,
a bestowal of unmerited advantage. Or perhaps it was because by the time
    I reached high school,

I was one hundred pounds and, to my father's dismay, would never be one
    hundred pounds
more than anyone, no matter how many chocolate milkshakes he pushed on me.
I asked my pediatrician once why I was so thin, if there was something wrong
    with me.
And this man who forced pills down my throat because I hadn't learned to
    swallow them,

who pricked my finger without warning to the point that I fainted, this man
    who seemed
to have no soul, replied so profoundly, so gently as I sat in my underwear on his
    exam table,
my feet dangling over the floor as if my lightness defied gravity,
That's the way God made you. You should love yourself the way you are.

Tonight, I stand before our bed in my boxers, hands on hips, and announce
I am going to begin lifting weights. That in a year from now I will be ripped
    like Jesus,
irresistible. But I know this isn't true. I know the difference between perception
    and reality,
the distorted image of myself I have fashioned in an effort to pass as formidable.

And as I stand there, weak but hopeful, an empty bowl I should fill with
    acceptance,
you smirk, reach for the switch of your bed lamp, and all my fantasies go dark.

Crying at Mount Saint Helens

If a man is going to cry,
let it be over a volcano,
something indelible
and dangerous,
which I didn't know
anyone else had done
until a man I met from Oregon
who had visited there too,
asked me if I'd cried as he had.

For him, it was thinking about all
the loss—
the trees like spilled matchsticks,
the volcanologist from the geological survey,
the retiree on Spirit Lake
who refused to evacuate,
who, before he perished, said,
It's part of me
and I'm part of that volcano.

I had been looking for the perfect
shot to hang in my office
when iron clouds rolled in
and rain drove the tourists
inside the visitor's center
where I had just bought a magnet
with a picture of the eruption
to stick on my refrigerator,
and which I held in a small plastic bag.

But it wasn't until I was alone
with it, until I was caught
by the open eye of it staring back,
that it happened,
that I felt like a shred in its time,
and not the other way around.

And I thought, if a religion was only this
it would be enough,
because there was nothing
between us. No window or lens.
Not even the word *volcano*.

Bill

Nice guy.
Vietnam vet.
Model citizen.
Strolls the block
in aviator sunglasses,
chin pointing up,
dog—small, white.
Waves to me
while I rake
fallen leaves,
which I will toss
into a dumping
area in the back
to rot and disappear.

I haven't seen Bill
pass by in a while.
The neighbor says
Bill's got stage four.
Stopped taking his pills.
Foreclosed on his house.
Locked himself inside.

We walk
our dogs—small, white.
Pause at Bill's house.
Dark like something dying.
Flag at half-mast.
Junk mail and fallen leaves
spilled across the lawn,
collecting in the hedges.
Unkempt, unlike Bill.
I wave my hand to say
the wind will clean it.
Nature takes care
of itself that way.
Makes things disappear.

Former soldiers.
Model citizens.
Nice guys.
Like Bill.

Pocket Change

It was the first thing he put
into his pocket in the morning

and the last thing he scattered
onto his dresser at night—

frozen profiles of presidents
staring into a shroud of darkness,

into each corner of his bedroom,
watching over him while he slept.

It paid for a newspaper,
a pack of cigs.

It called his wife to say he was running late,
covered the fare for the bus ride home.

It was proof of his daily toil,
the residue of broken dollars.

Sometimes, he used it to offset his accumulating more of it,
to reduce, but not to eliminate it entirely.

Otherwise, there would be nothing left of him.
Nothing to speak to the ways in which he provided.

Or, at the very least, nothing for his hand to do
while waiting for the early evening bus,

a four-noted instrument for his fingers to play,
jangling a restless, solo strain.

Canine Study #2: A Good Lieutenant

Each morning, he shakes
himself off in a contained fit—
a full body spasm,
a resetting,
as if forgetting everything
he has known—
before pulling into the grass
and squatting.

How predictable we are,
captives to our routine, he and I.
He is lost in concentration,
a breeze blowing the wisps of his ears,
his eyes half-closed
as if there were nothing
more satisfying than relieving oneself.

That, and having someone
who loves you unconditionally,
perhaps because his face
reminds me of my own,
or because his paw
seems to encompass
the pain of all the world.

As he straddles the road verge,
a throb of cars passes us,
heaving into the labor of the day.
Like a good lieutenant,
I pull a clean bag from my pocket.
This is what it must be like
to have nothing but your body,
I think, squatting behind him.
To be only what you are.

The Wolves under the House

He dropped out of college to marry her.
She sacrificed her thread of spontaneity.

He would give her a son and a daughter.
She would give him a home and a mortgage.

The wolf of him—
his den and chair.
The wolf of her—
her kitchen and stove.

One day he came home from work
and ate another chicken she baked.
He couldn't recall a thing before dinner
and recoiled at the tomorrow
she held in the corners of her mouth.
He was still speaking in code.
She had begun speaking in clouds.

The night after she left him,
he lost a thumbnail.
He planned to reattach it,
so he picked it off his pillow
and placed it on his nightstand.
The next morning, he lost the whole thumb.
Eventually his fingers were gone,
which made sense since he couldn't recall
the last time he had touched her.
Next were his genitals,
which he would have liked to keep
for someone else perhaps.
Then his arms, his legs,
everything except his head.

Odds were they wouldn't last.
They had said this to each other in passing.
He heard himself saying this now
to his coworkers and neighbors
when they inquired about his body.

They had fallen in love with their best intentions.
Not the rugged edges of their words
or the burr of their resentment,
but the wolves under the house.
The danger they thought they could tame.

Dream of Doves

for Benjamin, January 28, 2012

Today your father and I loaded
your first twin mattress
into the back of his minivan,
hauled it upstairs to your room
and placed it in the bedframe
that once held his first mattress.

Your mother spread a new comforter
with toy planes while, behind her,
jets sliced paths in the blue sunlight
across the transom high in the foyer.

At the park, your feet
dangled beneath the monkey bars
like two birds propelling you into boyhood.

At the air museum with you on my shoulders,
a wingspan wider than your eyes,
the Enola Gay hung, suspended
like a shiny bullet in a black and white memory
while a docent replied to questions adults asked—
the weight of bombs and exothermic reactions.

On the way home,
I checked on you in your car seat.
A thumb in your mouth,
the other hand under your shirt,
your index finger pressed into your belly button
as if to relieve some pressure.

Someday, I will explain life to you in terms of flying,
as a cycle of take-offs and landings.
I will say how we are the planes
and their intentions,

and how, after the rattle and hum of the day,
we shed our incidental cargo,
fold ourselves into bed
and dream of doves,
their silver, papery wings.

Before You Were Here

for Beth

Dad points out the unicorn
in the empty lot along Jordan Lane.
He does this every Saturday night
on the way to my grandparents' house.
Everyone pretends to see it except me.

When we arrive, Grandma pulls
our wrists into the kitchen.
A bowl of Chex Mix and a deck of Bicycle cards
on the table. A Benson and Hedges
dangling between her lips.

Downstairs at Grandpa's bar,
Ro pours air martinis for me and Steven.
She tops them off with invisible olives.
We toast and drink them down in one gulp.

Dad calls for us and we stumble upstairs,
tripping over each other like we're drunk.
He stands behind Mom,
his hands on her shoulders,
and announces we're having a baby.

Grandpa goes to the liquor cabinet
for a bottle of champagne.
His twelfth grandchild.
They are cheaper by the dozen, he says.

We feel Mom's stomach for a bump.
Grandma calls into it,
promises to spoil you rotten.
Steven and Ro make a bet
about whether you're a boy or a girl.
They tell me I will have to burp you
and change your dirty diapers.

On the way home,
a full moon follows our car.
As we pass the lot again,
Dad asks if I can see the unicorn.
When I tried to draw a picture of God once,
I drew a sunflower.
Now, I squint into the dark
and imagine you.
A shimmering body and legs.
A radiant head
nodding.

Sex Ed, or the Thing My Parents Were Doing

Age 9

I tell my friend Paul that my mother is pregnant.
He bellows over my head into each corner of the playground,
I know what your parents have been doing!
Paul carries a mustard satchel with a drawing
of a man and woman on a motorcycle—
her arms are around his waist,
he is looking confidently ahead—
as if being in love simply requires forward motion
and an urge Paul seems to understand too well for a fifth-grader.

Age 10

At the hospital's nursery window with my aunt,
I ask how they can tell whether my baby sister
is a boy or a girl.
She pats me on the head
and tells me to ask my parents.

Age 11

In health class, Kerry reads the magical phrase
over the collective breath of our sixth-grade classroom,
The man inserts his penis into the woman's vagina,
and you can almost hear the sound
of our adolescent doors unlocking.

Age 12

My friend shows me a magazine
he hides inside of a *Boy's Life* under his bed.
As he flips through the glossy pictures,
he asks me to push out my hips
so he can gauge my level of arousal.

Age 13

I listen to my brother's rock music
on the turntable in his room.
I scan the photographs inside his albums—
the landscape of the lead singer's bare chest,
his leather pants poised just above his pubic area,
his mouth frozen open in what could pass

as either pain or ecstasy.
Behind him, the band is doubled over their instruments.
The outstretched hands of the crowd reach
for them from the darkness.

Age 14

At dinner, my father asks if there are any girls I like.
I consider the Farrah Fawcett poster above my friend's bed,
then Danielle from school in her tight brown corduroys.
Kelly from church, I tell him,
having spoken to her only once,
not knowing if she even knows my name.
Ooh, do I hear wedding bells? he calls out to my mother.
As he says this, I sink into my chair—
an ache of a boy,
a gathering confusion,
this adolescent vortex
I will withstand on my own.

Day Care Report

for Ella, December 21, 2015

You won't remember crying at naptime yesterday,
or soaking your sleeves while washing your hands,
or how apple juice leaked from your bottle
and dripped into your boots.

When I sat at my desk this morning
and read your day care report,
the sun peeked beneath
the porch awning into my eyes.

I have always anticipated daylight's
rise from the ashes of December,
like ancient tombs in Ireland
whose entrances were positioned
so that light might pierce
their inner chamber
for a few fleeting moments
each winter solstice.

What if all we have of a day
is the sunlight captured in stone?
The recounting of a day care report?
If so, I wish you ones
with no more weight
than you can bear—
with restful sleep,
a clean, dry shirt
and a well-sealed bottle—
knowing that tomorrow will be
a little longer,
a little brighter.

Barber Shop: Things a Boy Should Do

Wait quietly, flipping through a sports magazine until the barber calls his name.

Remember to keep his head still each time the barber grunts and forces it into place.

Watch clippings fall like quotation marks over his cape and think how he will always be growing.

Appreciate the barber's humming because work can be both enjoyable and monotonous.

Tighten his temples against the straight blade the barber uses to even his sideburns.

Connect the red stripe in the barber pole to the blood flowing like rivers inside of him.

Relax his face under a warm towel as if he too, needs time to unwind like his father after work.

Tip for good service because the boy has always been the beneficiary of kindness.

Not look up when the barber pretends to toss him a piece of gum, but instead keeps it in his hand.

Ask politely if he can use the bathroom in back because the walk home is too far.

Survey the glossy poster on the bathroom door of a topless woman leering back at him.

Try to dismiss the image of the woman he now carries as he nods goodbye to the barber.

Not tell his parents about the woman, for fear they will think he is vulnerable or complicit.

Never speak of his desires, because it will take years before he will own his emotions.

Never speak of his desires.

Never speak.

School of Swimming

The school's name was a misnomer.
I don't recall learning to swim
or acquiring the slightest antidote
to my fear of the water.
The instructor had mastered
the art of coercion,
once tossing my unsuspecting body
from the diving board
after I hesitated jumping
into the deep end—
my limbs like cardinal points
smashing through the glassy surface.

A few summers later,
I took lessons from a lifeguard in town
who was tall and tanned
and happened to live on my street.
She wore a red one-piece with GUARD
written in white swells across her chest,
and was eighteen years to my ten.
I thought I could have her
if she would just wait for me
to reach high school,
or perhaps if I could impress her enough
by contorting my arms and legs
into consummating
the perfect breaststroke.

Each night after dinner,
I rode my new ten-speed around the block
again and again past her house,
much the way my parents
prayed the Rosary before bedtime—
one Our Father, ten Hail Marys, five times over—
believing that God favored the devout,
that petitions were granted for the sake of repetition,

and that, just once, as I pedaled by,
I would look into a window
and see Ann gazing back at me
through the blinds,
waving.

Stations of the Cross

It was the closest I would ever get to Maggie,
the eighth-grade beauty playing Mary to my Jesus
in our school's presentation of the fourth Station of the Cross—
a freeze frame of Jesus meeting his mother.

She is kneeling before me in a sky-blue robe
and white mantle. She has a look of compassion on her face,
which I would like to interpret as infatuation
rather than false sympathy for my impending crucifixion.

During rehearsal, Sister Grace suggested I rest my hand
on Maggie's head, and now my palm is sweating, quivering
because I can't help but think about how I am touching her
when I should be focused instead on saving humanity.

I wanted to put down my cardboard cross and confess
to my classmates and their families my feelings for Maggie,
despite how she paid me no more attention than on the day before.
I would have told them I was beginning to appreciate Jesus more,

that he wasn't loved in return either. I would have explained
how saviors and boys are mostly misunderstood,
how I had given myself over to an emotion that showed no mercy, how, tomorrow,
I would have no choice but to pick up my cross, spread my arms, and die.

Onions

or whatever you detest,
for no good reason.

Something inconsequential—
like red roses
or crows—
regardless of what others say.

There's onion in everything, Dad would chide.
And my mother, *You can't even taste onions.*
You're Italian-American, a friend once said. *They love onions.*

More recently, I have come to adore dogs,
the pause of Sunday evening,
even a day of good rain.

Someday, I may love onions
the way I love cilantro
or reading the first page of a novel.

But what if what we love is inbred,
a matter of geometry,
one shape over another

like the angle of jawline,
proof of cheekbone,
ratio of eyes to nose to lips?

How else do I explain
the way I give myself to something,
how I fall face-first into it,

headlong, to the point of ingestion,
to the point of such inexplicable
communion?

My Roommate, Reading

You could call it a fancy,
a fetish,
the way he, before reading,
would open a book,
lean in slowly,
eyes half-closed,
and press his nose
into the parted binding
for a semantic inhalation,
a little literary foreplay,
as if narrowing the gap between
meaning and comprehension,
and after a few breaths
lie back on his pillow,
the book hovering above him,
and gaze into the black
and white of its eyes,
caressing its lines,
the curves of its consonants,
and with deft fingers
turn its pages
as if unbuttoning a bodice,
sliding the straps from its shoulders,
devouring word after beautiful word.

We Won You

The morning after his favorite team had beaten mine,
Tommy would come to my locker to rub it in my face.
We won you, he said, which irritated me so much
I couldn't think clearly enough to correct his diction.

Such were the sports we pledged allegiance to,
the mockery we willingly endured,
our loyalties in the hands of men
who couldn't have cared less whether we wore their jerseys
or cheered for them from our living room sofas.

As Catholic school boys, we were a mixed bag—
fallen, cursed, defiant,
chosen, saved, forgiven—
the progeny of adults for whom life
was too short for skepticism.

The crusade of colors and logos we wore
was another form of prayer,
like wishing for outcomes beyond our control,
petitions we balanced between folded hands
and contrite hearts.
We should have known Jesus was just a metaphor,
like the athletes we idolized,
incarnations of our highest potential.

A priest once turned to the last page of the Bible
and declared us the winners.
But who was keeping score, I wondered?
If Anthony is the patron saint of lost things,
then who is the patron saint of losers,
or of people like Tommy and me,
those who lost by association?

Driving Range

Like monks in a scriptorium
leaning into their labor,
we are a perfect row of men,
each in his own hitting bay,
an oasis of concentration—
legs shoulder-width apart,
hands below the chin,
gripping the club gently
as if holding a bird.

Except for the occasional grunt,
feathered curse,
or sigh of disapproval,
we have taken a vow of silence.

We should have mastered it by now—
a simple rotation of the shoulders and hips,
a half-orbit around a white, dimpled sphere.
Each ball is a petition,
an agent of self-worth
we launch into this graveyard
of lofty expectations.

From a distance, one would wonder
what we are trying to prove—
a defiance of gravity,
a delaying of the inevitable descent to earth.
But we have our own definitions
of madness. Every swing closer
to the ten thousand required for mastery.

Hitting a golf ball should be easier than this,
easier than balancing a mortgage and marriage.
And sometimes it is,
like the times it feels effortless,
when the actor and action become one,
the way love feels at first,

the tiny moon of a man
rising above the tree line,
cresting into an arc of satisfaction,
a confluence of toil and desire
he points to and says,
Look. Look what I can do.

Removing a Stubborn Spike from a Golf Shoe

Its stuckness is by design,
a threaded screw and cone,
male and female.
Think of a lug nut on a wheel.
The very resistance I relied on for stability
was resisting my need to replace it.

My instinct dictated brute force—
untwist the spike into submission
the way a boy would pin another's arm
behind his back until he said *uncle*.
But this only causes the head of the spike to strip,
nothing for the metal removal tool to sink its teeth into.

Calling my father is a last resort.

WD-40, he says.

On a golf spike?

Trust me.

And, after the spraying,
and letting the slick
settle into the bore,
then twisting again,
the spike complies.

A molar coming loose.

Better to work smart than to work hard,
he says before saying goodbye,
an adage I imagine the men of his day abided by
after climbing into their pants each morning.
Men of responsibility and obligation,
of gumption and savvy.
Men, even, of knuckles
and brass tacks.

Canadian Mist

The whiskey ad in my monthly golf magazine
tells me, *Lighten up, this is going to be easy,*
though I can't help but notice the incongruity
of two men in an aluminum rowboat
a little offshore from a putting green.

The snow-capped mountain looming
in the distance is difficult to ignore, as is
the superimposed image of a giant bottle
and two glasses of golden liquor on ice floating
along with the men on the pond.

Perhaps it wasn't enough to tell colleagues
how they skipped work to play golf.
Their story needed a boat without oars,
like modern-day apostles forsaking
their possessions and pushing off into a watery
subconscious, until they became as misplaced
as shots of whiskey on a golf course.

Or perhaps playing golf was a figment of their imaginations,
the haze of another week of working, commuting,
and finally, on Sunday, falling asleep on the couch
to the whisper of a golf tournament on TV,
a bottle of whiskey on the end table—
a glimmer in a living room that is too dim
over a life that is the wrong shade of green
and a weekend that is always a day short.

Learning to Dunk

I guaranteed my friend I'd do it within a year.
I must have been feeling my oats, as my parents said,

or flirting with the deadly sin of pride, as my teachers warned.
But wasn't that the point? To defy my natural boundaries,

to crack the secret domain of God,
the hallowed air of the ten-foot-high rim?

A boy is nothing unless he is functional,
a man in training who can run and lift and jump.

For years, as if on instinct, I had been grazing ceiling tiles
with my fingertips, slapping door lintels with my palms.

I began to lose interest in basketball the first time I fell in love.
Funny, this falling I embraced, the inverse of pride, the ground taken out
    from under me.

But even this felt like flying, the only dream I can remember,
the one where I propel myself over treetops simply by kicking my feet.

Today, I resisted the urge to jump and touch an exit sign.
I recalled the boy I lost, still learning to dunk, still hoping to fall.

Batting Cage

Each time he swung and missed—
his body unwound
in a posture of spent effort—
it was as if his father
had vanished again.

And the times he connected—
the sting of the bat in his spleen—
was some recompense for every year
he had stayed home
to care for his mother.

But there was something feeble
about the violence of his hits—
his loosened chin,
the ache in his arms,
the ball slackening
into the netting as if to say
it had been hit harder
by more imposing men,
fatherless men too,
before falling
to the batting cage floor
and gazing back at him
with its red-stitched smirk.

Drawing the Tree

The picture
he drew
of his childhood
was the maple
he climbed,
a respite
from the turmoil
on the ground—
the broken machines
of the day
and the father
who beat
a path
to the garage
searching
for the tools
to fix them.

His father took the tree
down one day
without warning
or explanation—
the earthen heart
of its upturned stump
and dismembered
limbs strewn
across the yard
like dead soldiers.

As he grew,
the tree became
one more thing
he was deprived of.
An object of his
father's combustion.
How little his father
knew about him,

all the climbing
he still had to do,
to look down
from above his house
wearing a crown
of leaves,
depths of sky
to fathom.

Some Branch

This incessant state of childhood
    a stack of disappointments to reconcile.

The promises your father withheld
    his elusive acknowledgement

despite all the potential of him
    the tree of his sternum

the blue above his boughs
    his limbs you climbed for fruit.

The person you have become
    is it like him?

Perhaps you are simply the residue of his labor
    the consequence of his hands.

If he gave his approval to you now
    with outstretched arms

as if some branch
    as if you were more than your accomplishments

would you cradle it in your arms
    careful not to spill its marrow?

Would it abide in your chest?
    Would you allow yourself to rest there?

The Day after Her Birthday

The eye of summer will make
its way again across her bedroom,
scan the primal landscape of sleep—
a petulant alarm clock,
tossed underwear adorning
a stack of mysteries,
an ammonite pendant
from a shop at the beach yesterday
and a bowl of seashells in mid whorl—
angel wing, cut ribbed ark, cockle, conch.

Today will want for nothing.
She will not compensate
for what it may lack
or cut its light into shadows,
its hours into expectation.

She will die a little today,
shed her layers of regret
and expose the soft
mollusk of her body.
She will flick the galaxies of sand
from between her toes.
The age that has wedged
itself in the back of her mind,
she will strip of its pretension,
twist it into submission.

Tonight, when the stars bear the sky,
she will name a new constellation
within its ocean.
She will call it
indifferent,
fortuitous,
wonderful.

Endearments

If you ponder some of the names
you've been called throughout your life—
brash indignities and innocuous insults
you shielded with the hard part of your brain—
maybe *sugar, sweetie,* and *honey*
aren't so patronizing
coming from the manager
of the burrito place you stop into
on your way home from work
as she hands you a soda cup,
your change, and your receipt—
her gentle ellipses at the end of every platitude
dressing up the verbal tics of customer service.

And in the small space
of an ordinary business transaction,
you believe she is sincere
simply because her endearments
are kinder than most of the names
you've been called.
More bonhomie than impertinent.
Nothing like the language
of hammers and screwdrivers
they spoke back home,

but more like the way you imagine they speak
during coffee hour after church—
the rise and fall of pleasantries
between bites of powdered donuts—
a religious inflection to carry into Monday.
Or the way you imagine they speak
in a town far south of here,
a place you plan to visit someday
where strangers are greeted with a drawl
and people hold doors open for each other,
where the beach is just down the road
and it is always summer.

Tourists

We stop at a roadside pottery store
for a piece of Jamaica to take back
to our cruise ship in the bay.
The potter smiles behind his wheel,
pumps the pedal, binds soft earth.
He says making pottery is like giving birth
and holds up a newborn piece for our cameras.

Outside, someone points to a nude beach
in the distance dotted with thatched cabanas.
We step closer to the edge of a cleft
to gaze at the fleshy figures floating across sand,
mirages perhaps, though we know well
the tones of bare skin, the contour
of the body like so many vases and mugs.

I imagine the potter having coffee with his wife tonight.
He will describe the tourists with a word like *nudity*,
while we carry bittersweet souvenirs
beneath a warm moon
amid the buoyancy of a cruise.
We will crave beautiful things we can't buy.
The potter's hands.
The shape of air between them.

Stopping by a Southern Town

Consider the ways the day is circular.

You buy a silk infinity scarf
at the consignment store.

We spin on stools at the soda fountain,
dip silver spoons into frosted bowls of ice cream.

The rotary in the center of town
yields a steady stream of traffic.

On it, a statue to Confederate heroes
rises into the afternoon like a granite fist.

Even the soldier's mouth is rounded
as if he were awakened from a long slumber.

A town has a way of turning
in on itself, of clinging to anonymity.

Behind the monument is the county courthouse
and a pole with a crisp American flag.

The cars orbit around these too.
Their wheels spin without making a sound.

Shakshuka

Tomato sauce, beans, and eggs—
    a new recipe for dinner,

foreign to my eyes and tongue
    because this year I have resolved

to step outside my comfort zone,
    beyond the radius of work and home,

perhaps as far as Maghreb
    where I learn shakshuka originates

and which I peruse images of now
    imagining myself walking along a narrow alley

of doors as ornate and varied as the faces of humanity,
    stopping before one—

a shade of blue, a cross between royal and azure,
    like the summer sky of childhood,

sunburst transom above,
    thin clouds of mosaic trim around—

and picking up the utensils of adventure
    and knocking, not because I know what is behind it,

but because, for once, I am content
    not knowing a thing.

Forty

If life is a rubber band and you
are the hand that is stationary,
then forty is the other hand
that has slowly pulled away,

a cruise ship rolling through warm water,
a hot universe expanding
leaving traces of you under rugs
and fingernails and other dark places.

Some will nod their heads and smile
knowing that you are forty
and are simply stretching your legs,
and that you will come back to yourself

just as gradually as you departed,
like grace settling into a white cottage
with gingham curtains and a picket fence.
A place that has been vacant too long.

Token Priest

It was my grandmother's dying wish
as she cradled the crystal ball
of my teenage head in her hands.
Become a priest, honey.
You would make such a wonderful priest for our family.

I was the last prospect on the small branch
she had sprouted—
the youngest male child of her youngest child,
a beacon of purity in the fallen world
of afternoon soap operas
she watched religiously
while knitting.

She was the epitome of sanctity,
the guiding light of our family
and a devoted widow who, each day,
shuffled through holy cards of the saints
like those of the baseball players I collected.

Perhaps she was protecting me from everything
I couldn't have known,
that priesthood would be less grueling
than the strange coupling she had undertaken,
the same simmering desire
that would propel my unsuspecting
body into adulthood.

She must have confused me
for a grandchild whose will was expendable,
who would sacrifice in order to bestow
supernatural favor on the family.
But how I prayed her last wish for me
was simply for my happiness,
to hand me her needles
and commission me
to knit the yarn of her affection
into contentment.

Omniscient Sea

1900. The year you were born,
Grandma. You said you went
with the years, so I always
knew how old you were.

1980. Seeing you in Florida.
My first plane ride.
Isn't it ironic
that I was closer to Heaven,
but scared to death of falling?

Summers. You came back north.
When I visited, you offered me
the cookies you made. You said
you were tired of living. I didn't
think someone holding a tray of
pizzelle could be so sad. You asked
if I was going to Mass and I lied.
God knows everything you do, you said.
Don't make him cry.

1996. September. The day
of your funeral
it rained. That October,
I was married on a beach.
It rained that day too.
This refrain of water. Raindrops
scattered across your casket.
God's tears in an omniscient sea.

Canine Study #3: Two Bulbs

It could take
my lifetime
to understand him,

how there is no distinction
between who he is
and what he does.

Meanwhile, I am returning
to the Self
which Jung spoke of.

For all I know
we are vials of energy,
two bulbs,

as each evening
he stops me outside
to sit on the steps,

and I think
how there are more stars
than grains of sand on earth.

Ten times
my grandparents spun
dust into light.

Tonight, I fathom
one star,
contemplate this dog.

Cleanliness

It is next to Godliness, they say,
like the Sunday afternoon I saw my aunts
in the unbearable heat of that summer
stripped down to their underwear
cleaning the house their sister had just bought,
which my mother described as a God-awful mess.

It was a photo negative of how my pre-teen eyes
were accustomed to seeing them—
a jigsaw puzzle of skin and girlish under-habit,
the ivory sweep of their shoulders, navels, and thighs
as they stood on step ladders and chairs,
bent over boxes and twisted into corners and nooks.

Difficult to imagine then, that beneath their piety
were the gentle landscapes of their bodies—
the primal vessels of my cousins,
the loose ends of them rippling in delayed reaction
to the back and forth motion of their arms.
A femininity that was at once confusing and alluring.

If our souls are on loan to us from God,
as we were taught,
then all that was tangible of my aunts
must have been theirs—
the parts I imagined my uncles
traced with their hands at night
as they peeled back layers of darkness.

Besides, I had never known God
to reconcile nakedness and attraction,
the body's function with its form.
For all we were told he could do,
I had never known him to consummate flesh.
Never seen him give birth.

Mother, Planting

Her back is tired
from planting bulbs
all afternoon—
tulip, daffodil, crocus.
She moves slowly,
like hands pressing
into thick soil.

How restless
the seasons can be.
She has been ill
and has suffered
these past few
with grace.

It would be easy
to mistake
her perseverance
for devoutness,
to credit God
for the ordinary miracles
she performs.

But redemption stirs
in her garden.
Faith in seeds.
Life wanting to live.
My conception
a mystery
to everyone but her.

Invisible Roots

Let's talk in marigolds, Mother,
like the orange and yellow blooms
you planted along the stone wall back home
where I sat and posed
on my first day of grade school.
My crisp Oxford you ironed, and clip-on tie,
a White Owl cigar box of school supplies
in my lap, and Buster Browns on my feet.

You knew to capture the moment
before the school bus came.
Standing over me in the driveway,
a halo of sun above your head,
you asked me to smile for the camera
while I squinted in the light,
head cocked, legs crossed.

I wonder what you thought that day
in the mother's clothes you wore.
Was it how to fill the fresh silence of a house?
Or finding a name for something you lost?

When the bus,
imminent as a bloom,
turned onto our street
and I stood up to leave,
did you sense too,
the invisible roots between us
stretching thin through the lens?

A Defense of Poetry

"Fool," said my muse to me, "look in thy heart and write."
~ Sir Philip Sidney, A Defense of Poetry

Because the night sky
has trillions of ways
of whispering *Yes.*

Because a longleaf pine
contains immeasurable
silence.

Because *tulip*
is another way
of saying *now.*

Because the body
has many rooms
for joy.

Because the daily bread
we bless
is instead, blessing us.

Autotomy

For their wedding anniversary
she asked for a door—
forest green,
with a window
to let the light in
and to warm the dog
curled in the foyer.

After he installed it—forest green,
a window, just as she had asked—
a man came knocking.
He extended a tract to her
and asked where she finds comfort.
She looked beyond him
and pointed to an anole
sunning itself on a railing.
She slid the tract from his fingers
because she was kind.

The next Saturday,
the man knocked again.
She watched him through the window.
There had been a steady rain
and he had no hat or umbrella.
He waved a bible
in front of her like an indulgence
and said he wanted to talk
about how she could grow closer to God.

She smiled as if to pity him,
Did you know anoles have autotomic tails?

He looked at her, perplexed.

Their tails fall off when they're attacked, she explained,
and then they grow new ones.

But what about God? he said.

Yes, she said,
God.

Our Feet

Yours and mine,
like couples
double-dating,
first meeting
under a table
in a college cafeteria,
their muffled
exchange underneath
our teenage voices.

They share
a common geometry—
parallel,
perpendicular,
intersecting,
but mostly oblique.

They are mirror opposites.

Tonight, they are
performing a domestic waltz,
half-circling
a stove,
preparing dinner,
a hungry dog
between them.

We should have
a talk with our feet.
Ask them to remind us
what they admire
about each other,
for the times we forget.

They must be naïve,
these feet.
How else to explain
their blind obedience,
their quiet defiance?

Think of the labyrinths
they have traced
together.
Their contradictory
sense of harmony.
How they both
lead and follow.

Where Eternity Begins

No, you said.

I was pointing
beyond the fingertips
of the longleaf pines
swaying in heaven above us.

You genuflected
and held your palm
over the face
of a dandelion.

Here.

Skipping Stone

The weekend after you lost
your job, we drove one hundred

miles to the Atlantic,
held hands along the boardwalk

and shuffled through sand
before you paused

and pondered the waves,
then bent over for a stone,

smooth and flat, aerodynamic
like the ones I was taught

to skip sidearm like a relief pitcher,
a motion I didn't realize you could make,

and, with determined lips,
you swung through and held your stance

as the stone shot high off a whitecap,
flickered, then hung as if wounded

before plummeting into an ocean
as nebulous as a job,

and when you released your grimace
and took my hand again,

I wondered if the stone
felt something of your pain

when it landed on the cold,
implacable floor.

Skeleton Key

Breakfast at an inn this summer—
four couples perfectly paired
around the orange tongues
of candles, the crystal fingers of
knife-rests on a white tablecloth.
We talk of our accomplishments,
of the ambitions of grown children.

On the porch that night,
a couple tells me of the recent passing
of their son,
a disease that paid no mind
to his young family and promising career.
It seems their grief is lost
somewhere between them
and they have been trying
to find their separate ways to it.

Upstairs, each guest room
has its own name and décor.
Even the floorboards emit
distinct groans under our shoes.
But I imagine the skeleton keys
for the others' door handles
are just as stubborn as ours,
until finally, I feel ours catch
and the latch gives way—
this wrought instrument
of mystery
and the quiet dwellings
of our solace and sorrow.

chi

the black between the stars
the sky around our house

the knife and white dish
the pineapple of our thoughts

the silence after we speak
the applause the trees make when we are quiet

the outline of empty space tonight
like a child between our sleeping bodies

Canine Study #4: Ten Thousand Things

I slip out of bed and onto the floor.

     Still human.

The dog walks over as I pour food into his bowl.

     Still canine.

Our silences this morning seem intertwined.

     Consciousness should feel like this.

Like good health.

     Like nothing.

No distinction.

     Between me.

And him.

     And the ten thousand things.

Breath Become a Gale

When my parents call during the hurricane,
one right after the other,
myself a thousand miles in between them,
it seems as if they have coordinated
their checking in on me.

When they ask about the gusts and rain,
whether there is flooding,
and say, *Where exactly do you live again?*
it isn't that they are worried for my safety.
They too, have been awakened by wind,
by rain pounding the drum skin of windowpanes.
It seems rather, they are recalling the work of their hands,
acknowledging the invisible person of me
they still carry.

When I hang up with one, then the other,
and stand on the porch to watch the storm
scratch its fingernails across the sky,
reaching behind while the angry head of it spirals northward,
it reminds me of the years they were together,
the infinite distance a couple must bridge,
and of my body—
the last part of them still conjoined,
a breath become a gale.

Vanity Plates

They are the go-getters—
MOM 26.2 and JUSDUIT—
while the rest of us just go.

They are N2HVNFUN,
see the CUP FULL, and they LIV4LUV,
while we are only living for the weekend.

They are the stop-light philosophers
who ask DOUXIST?
and like good parents, they assure us,
IHERDEWE, now GO2SLEEP.

They make us wish we had enough faith
to plaster SOLI DEO or JESUSWIL
across our backsides.

DONTFUSS, B GR8FUL, they remind us,
and, despite the drain of morning traffic,
they C2BHAPPY and say, it's OK2LAUGH.

They claim to be the R!NG LDR,
declare IM2MUCH,
and boast 2L8 IWUN to those of us
who are content to remain nameless,
who cluster in the field chewing grass all day,
amused enough to decipher their identities
in the space of eight characters,
noticing how, despite their eccentricities,
they are all heading in the same direction,
following each other along.

Catching Up with John

I e-mail John that I am coming to Boston for work and would he like to get together and maybe do something? I haven't seen him since college, and I'd like to catch up with him and see if he has the same lines around his eyes and graying temples that I have. We can reminisce about the time he dated the blonde he knew I liked in arts survey class. I offer to get a rental car so he won't have to pick me up. He says he has a lot to tell me and he misses college too and hasn't really made the effort to contact anyone since graduation.

After I arrive, I call John from the ice rink where my office is holding its Christmas party. I move into a stairwell where there is an echo, but away from the commotion of EMTs who are taking our quality assurance manager to the hospital after she tripped on the ice and dislocated her shoulder and maybe broke her wrist. John says I sound like I am inside a soup can and I keep saying *what* until I understand his daughter has a cough and besides, there is snow coming tonight and it may not be safe to drive and his wife is worried about everything lately.

Before we hang up, we say next time we will plan it better even though we can't control colds and spouses and the weather, and maybe we should call each other again sometime to chat. So I will walk around the city tonight and brush past people I don't know. I will pretend one of them is John and we will tie our best intentions together and go to a Thai restaurant where we will laugh over Christine, or was it Sarah, and notice how strangers on the sidewalk outside narrow their shoulders to avoid touching each other, while the complicated snow falls around them, while John and I stare through the flickering light of a candle and study the familiar patterns of our faces.

Fat and Happy

If someone you haven't seen in a while
asks how you have been,
don't say, *Fat and happy.*
Say what everyone says, *Oh, I've been busy.*
This will make you sound important,
so important that you don't have time
for lost acquaintances.

And before this person can ask
the things you are occupied with,
rather than forage your pockets for a lie,
clap him on the back and say,
I really have to get going.
Then walk briskly
to the cocoon of your car
or to the shelter of some building.

Look over your shoulder and say
how good it was to see him
and to give your best to so-and-so.
If you're feeling brave,
throw in, *We should get together,*
even though you are together now,
or were for a moment
until he dared to ask how you have been.

After all, you have an image
of diligence to uphold.
The last thing you want him to think
is that you are idle,
that you tend to overeat
and watch too much TV.
Or that you could simply be
happy.

God Bless America

A petition
and a command

as in,

      eyes see clearly

           ears listen intently

                hands touch tenderly

                     tongues speak thoughtfully

                minds think broadly

           parents raise lovingly

      children act kindly.

In other words,
Us bless us.

Enjoy Your Flight

Three words
conclude the attendant's safety demonstration.

The imperative *enjoy*—

as if the experience of every routine act
were a matter of perception.
As if enjoyment were a choice,
a state of mind.
As if how you do anything
is how you do everything.

The possessive *your*—

as if flying were a personal item,
a carry-on,
commonplace like breath.
As if the airplane was your body
whose simplest function is a mystery.
As if your life isn't already a miracle.

The direct object *flight*—

the same way the heart is an object,
or the brain,
the plane's and yours,
these fortunate accidents of departure and arrival
and the many things in a day to be grateful for.
Don't bother trying to make sense of it.

You will never understand it all.

Acknowledgments

Angel City Review: "Barber Shop: Things a Boy Should Do," "Drawing the Tree,"
   "Odd Camaraderie," "Smash It Up"
Chagrin River Review: "Last Request"
Cider Press Review: "Cleanliness"
Connecticut River Review: "Skeleton Key"
Hamilton Stone Review: "Dream of Doves," "Omniscient Sea," "The Wolves
   under the House"
Kakalak 2018: "The Day after Her Birthday," "Hitting the Deer"
Kakalak 2019: "Breath Become a Gale," "Endearments"
Hawaii Pacific Review: "Ode to a Couch"
Main Street Rag: "Pocket Change"
Prime Number Magazine: "Revenge Enough"
Redheaded Stepchild: "A River, Flowing"
South Florida Poetry Journal: "Tourists"
Sport Literate: "Driving Range," "We Won You"
Toasted Cheese: "Before You Were Here," "Day Care Report," "Invisible Roots,"
   "Stations of the Cross"
The Under Review: "God, Bowling," "Learning to Dunk"
Two Cities Review: "Dogs"

"Batting Cage," "Catching the Fish," and "Neighborhood Men" appeared in *Nazim Hikmet Poetry Contest Chapbook 2018* (Nazim Hikmet Poetry Festival, 2018).

"Bill" appeared in *North Carolina Bards, Raleigh Poetry Review: An Anthology of Poetry* (Local Gems Press, 2020).

"Mother, Planting" appeared in *New York Quarterly: Without a Doubt, poems illuminating faith* (New York Quarterly Books, 2022).

"Sex Ed, or the Thing My Parents Were Doing" appeared in *Pinesong: Awards 2018* (North Carolina Poetry Society, 2018).

"Skipping Stone" appeared in *Bards Against Hunger North Carolina: An Anthology of North Carolina Poets* (Local Gems Press, 2020).

"Stopping by a Southern Town" appeared in *Pinesong: Awards 2019* (North Carolina Poetry Society, 2019).

The following poems were selected for the annual North Carolina Poetry Society's *Poetry in Plain Sight* program: "Chi" (2018), "Where Eternity Begins" (2021), "A Defense of Poetry" (2022).

These poems have won awards: "Batting Cage," "Catching the Fish," and "Neighborhood Men" (Honorable Mention, 2018 Nazim Hikmet Poetry Contest); "Chemistry" (First Place, 2018 Flyleaf Books Poetry Contest); "Sex Ed, or the Thing My Parents Were Doing" (Honorable Mention, 2018 North Carolina Poetry Society Contest, Thomas H. McDill Award); "Stopping by a Southern Town" (Second Place, 2019 North Carolina Poetry Society Contest, Poetry of Witness Award).

"Learning to Dunk" was nominated for a 2021 Pushcart Prize.

About FutureCycle Press

FutureCycle Press is dedicated to publishing lasting English-language poetry in both print-on-demand and Kindle ebook formats. Founded in 2007 by long-time independent editor/publishers and partners Diane Kistner and Robert S. King, the press was incorporated as a nonprofit in 2012. A number of our editors are distinguished poets and writers in their own right, and we have been actively involved in the small press movement going back to the early seventies.

Each year, we award the FutureCycle Poetry Book Prize and honorarium for the best original full-length volume of poetry we published that year. Introduced in 2013, proceeds from our Good Works projects are donated to charity. Our Selected Poems series highlights contemporary poets with a substantial body of work to their credit; with this series we strive to resurrect work that has had limited distribution and is now out of print.

We are dedicated to giving all of the authors we publish the care their work deserves, offering a catalog of the most diverse and distinguished work possible, and paying forward any earnings to fund more great books. All of our books are kept "alive" and available unless and until an author requests a title be taken out of print.

We've learned a few things about independent publishing over the years. We've also evolved a unique and resilient publishing model that allows us to focus mainly on vetting and preserving for posterity poetry collections of exceptional quality without becoming overwhelmed with bookkeeping and mailing, fundraising activities, or taxing editorial and production "bubbles." To find out more about what we are doing, come see us at futurecycle.org.

The FutureCycle Poetry Book Prize

All original, full-length poetry books published by FutureCycle Press in a given calendar year are considered for the annual FutureCycle Poetry Book Prize. This allows us to consider each submission on its own merits, outside of the context of a traditional contest. Too, the judges see the finished book, which will have benefitted from the beautiful book design and strong editorial gloss we are famous for.

The book ranked the best in judging is announced as the prize-winner in January of the subsequent year. There is no fixed monetary award; instead, the winning poet receives an honorarium of 20% of the total net royalties from all poetry books and chapbooks the press sold online in the year the winning book was published. The winner is also accorded the honor of being on the panel of judges for the next year's competition; all judges receive copies of the contending books to keep for their personal library.

www.ingramcontent.com/pod-product-compliance
Lightning Source LLC
Chambersburg PA
CBHW070002100426
42741CB00012B/3105